Owen Seaman

Tillers of the Sand

Owen Seaman

Tillers of the Sand

ISBN/EAN: 9783744687935

Printed in Europe, USA, Canada, Australia, Japan

Cover: Foto ©Thomas Meinert / pixelio.de

More available books at **www.hansebooks.com**

TILLERS OF THE SAND

BEING A FITFUL RECORD OF

THE ROSEBERY ADMINISTRATION

FROM THE TRIUMPH OF LADAS TO THE
DECLINE AND FALL-OFF

BY

OWEN SEAMAN

AUTHOR OF
'HORACE AT CAMBRIDGE' AND 'WITH DOUBLE PIPE'

LONDON
SMITH, ELDER, & CO., 15 WATERLOO PLACE
1895

THESE desultory sets of verse, written from time to time in illustration of various episodes in Lord Rosebery's late Administration, have, with one exception, been already in print: the majority in 'The National Observer,' four in 'The World,' two in 'Punch.' I have to acknowledge the courtesy of the editors of 'The National Observer' and 'The World' in allowing me to reprint work that has appeared in their pages. For permission to use the two poems from 'Punch' I wish to thank Messrs. Bradbury, Agnew & Co., more especially that in the case of one of the poems they have made an exception to their rule requiring a fixed interval of time before republication.

O. S.

CONTENTS

—◦◆◦—

viii CONTENTS

DISSOLVING VIEWS

(A RADICAL MANIFESTO)

INTELLIGENT Electorate !
    I come commended by the Caucus ;
Their notion was that in debate
    My voice would prove extremely raucous ;
I naturally like to mention
My leading claim on your attention.

Far be it from me, I may add,
    To underrate my private merits,
But as a fact the Caucus had
    To burrow like a lot of ferrets,
And simply wriggle all they knew
To raise a candidate for you.

B

You pardonably drop a hint
  That I should answer certain questions,
And put, if possible, in print
  Some rough and tentative suggestions
To indicate our future rôle
In case we conquer at the poll.

I understand our noble Chief
  Would have the Peers annihilated ;
Another batch, we note with grief,
  Has recently been elevated ;
Why *does* he crown his own connection
Before he scalps the whole collection ?

' Down with the Union Jack ! ' says John ;
  'Down with the Church !' says Asquith; ' that 'll
Be found a useful malison
  To yell along the line of battle ; '

Amid the common shout for slaughter

Sir Wilfrid faintly calls for Water.

Apart from this portentous list,

 So damnatory and seductive,

We ought to meet the Unionist

 With schemes a little more constructive ;

At times the best of agitators

Are bound to pose as legislators.

We all possess dissolving views ;

 You pine, no doubt, to pinch your neighbours,

To rob the honest rich, and use

 The fruit of other people's labours ;

Expect me shortly on the spot,

I'll gladly undertake the lot.

4

THE PROMISE OF LADAS.

Who names this colt ?   What eponym

    Stands sponsor for his morals ?

I, Ladas, large and lithe of limb,

    Lord of a hundred laurels !

On whom the loud Olympic ring,

    Ignoring local squabbles

And every other mortal thing,

    Sat tight, and planked their obols.

Parsley and olive, palm and bay—

    Without exaggeration

I take it that I bore away

    A positive plantation ;

Till Elis saw me pass the post
    By just a bare priority,
And send my gallant, breathless ghost
    To join the great majority.

He, too, has joined their fighting ranks,
    The heir to my tradition ;
All on the downs his glossy·flanks
    Defy the Opposition ;
Sound as his owner's chosen make
    Of Government despatch-box,
Exploding prophecies that stake
    Their safety on a *Matchbox*..

As Myron set me up in bronze,
    To make my parish vainer,
May he through fortune's pros and cons
    Set up (in tin) his trainer ;

So may he, like the knowing ox,

Adorn his master's crib and

Avoiding spavins on his hocks

Take back the Turf's blue riband !

Go on, my noble king of steeds !

Go on, *virtute macte !*

Prime minister to all their needs

Who went and freely backed 'ee ;

And if there's really something in

Success that fans infection,

Who knows but what a triple win

Will turn the next election ?

Punch, May 19, 1894.

[Mr. Chamberlain quoted to the House from a letter of his hon. friend Sir W. Lawson to Mr. Whyte, Secretary of the United Kingdom Alliance, on the prospects of the Government Liquor Traffic (Local Control) Bill, in which he had said that Lord Rosebery declared the Temperance men to be the backbone of the Liberal Party. (Laughter.) ' Remember,' ran the letter, ' how gallantly Sir William Harcourt, who takes charge of the Bill, has nailed his colours to the mast.']

WHEN the Chief of the Exchequer

Had relieved his mental pecker

(He's the Champion we casually slight),

From the right-hand seat beside me

Some one ventured to deride me

For a letter that I wrote to Mr. Whyte.

It would seem that my effusions

Often bristle with allusions

To the victory of Water and the Right ;

For it is my joy to see to

The success of Local Veto,

And I clearly said the same to Mr. Whyte.

Clearly told my gentle reader

That our battle-breathing Leader

Was in admirable fettle for the fight ;

That he'd sport the true-blue riband,

Quaff a rousing Cocoa Nib, and

Rally round the ranks of me and Mr. Whyte.

Though the ship of State were leaking,

He would—nautically speaking—

Nail our colours to the masthead, trim and tight ;

    And desert the sorry pennants

    Of the late Evicted Tenants

('Though I kept the latter dark from Mr. Whyte).

    Nay, the Premier in hearty

    Terms had hinted that our party

Was his 'backbone,' and a source of much delight :

    But he's either dislocated,

    Or become invertebrated,

Since I quoted the above to Mr. Whyte.

    It may be the rise in whisky

    Made the Bill a little risky,

In the case of ardent spirits feeling spite ;

    And our publicans and sinners,

    Like the best of Derby winners,

Might have rounded on myself and Mr. Whyte.

I am not, of course, a racer,

I have never found it pay, sir,

But I'm bound to own a sort of sense of blight,

Since the sad Eclipse of Ladas

Caused the Liberal hopes to fade as

Fade the leaves—of letters sent to Mr. Whyte.

Once our cause was fairly in it,

'Growing stronger every minute'—

That's the phrase that I selected to indite ;

Now it's weak as toast and water,

Though perhaps I didn't oughter

Name a beverage beloved of Mr. Whyte.

When our Head demurely mentions

His proverbial intentions,

And observes in language really rather trite,

That it still will be his pleasure

To 'push forward' with the measure,

Why, we beg to doubt it, don't we, Mr. Whyte?

I dislike to be facetious,

But I think the promise specious,

And I say a party cuts a sorry sight,

Straining every other jack bone

With a jelly for its 'backbone,'

Which is what we've been reduced to, Mr. Whyte.

National Observer, July 28, 1894.

A LITANY IN TIME OF NEED

(Evicted Tenants Bill)

FROM the pestilent, privy sedition
  Whose hand is at honesty's throat,
From the bane of a Party's ambition
  Whose soul is on sale for a vote ;
From the snare of the impudent fowler,
  From treachery sharper than swords,
From the latest political howler—
      Defend us, good Lords !

From a Ministry's dodge that is drastic
  For gagging the gorge of dissent,
From the Leaguers whose law is elastic
  On rent and the paying of rent ;

From the rule that the wretches who do so
  Be badgered by boycotting hordes,
Crying ' Ho ! for O'Brien his trousseau ! '—
      Defend us, good Lords !

When integrity proves suicidal,
  And honour is seared with a brand ;
When the labour on land that is idle
  Is known as the grabbing of land ;
When a curse is on faithful endeavour,
  And Parliament keeps its rewards'
For the breach of a bond—then, if ever,
      Defend us, good Lords !

From the scheme for a national bounty
  Releasing America's dole
Broadcast over borough and county,
  To sweeten the path to the poll ;

From irregular raising of riches

  To amplify alien hoards

By the broaching of Englishmen's breeches—

      Defend us, good Lords !

From the sham elegiacs of mealy-

  Mouthed agents of Ireland's woes,

From the efforts of Timothy Healy

  To sever the shamrock and rose,

From the scare that the Government gave us

  When loyalty went by the boards—

You have saved us already, O save us

      Now also, good Lords !

Such a grace we will gladly remember

  When Radical talkers renew

The design for a Fifth of November

  Exclusively levelled at you ;

For the nation will never dishonour

A debt that she duly records,

And, if asked, she will take it upon her

To save you, my Lords !

National Observer, August 18, 1894.

THE BITTER CRY OF THE PRIVATE MEMBER

O WALY, waly, up the House !

    And waly, waly, down again !

And waly for the butchered Bills,

    The little Bills we backed in vain !

I leaned my weight unto an oak

    —This venerable plant is here

Put for a Ministerial pledge—

    It broke : the shock was most severe.

It's not the dearth of holidays,

    Though they have been extremely few ;

Nor yet the wicked waste of time,

    Though this is irritating too ;

It's not the ventilation of
   The House, though that is rather crude ;
What really hurts a Member's health
   Is Ministers' ingratitude.

O promises are mighty fine,
   And fine the flattery of whips,
But when you reach the net result
   'Tis but a windy meal of pips ;
O wherefore did I plank my vote
   For grist to yonder Party mill ?
For now my Leader lets me down
   And suffocates my little Bill.

When we came in by London town
   Our hearts were high with hope and joy ;
Some of us wore the tartan kilt,
   And some the hardy corduroy :

We played the crofter's reel and sang
  The coster's dirge of discontent ;
And when we piped the Party danced,
  And when we mourned they made lament.

But now that we have saved the game,
  And served the Session's public need,
Whether we pipe, or mourn, or both,
  They simply pay no sort of heed ;
But had we guessed our private quest
  Would end in such a sickly sell,
A dozen of us might have struck
  And sent the Budget Bill to h——.

Now Arthur's seat I'll sit behind,
  Carouse with ever-flowing Bowles,
And simulate the ' busy bee '
  With other transmigrating souls ;

I'll wave the rebel rag of Weir,

    Roost in the wild Macgregor's 'cave,'

Go pander to the Parnellite,

    And generally misbehave.

O waly, waly, up the House !

    And waly, waly, down again

(I've used the phrase before, and still

    The meaning's very far from plain) !

For O, if my true little Bill

    Were yet alive, and looking fit !

But now it's in the common grave,

    Green grass already over it.

National Observer, August 25, 1894.

SOMNUS AGRESTIUM ;

OR, THE BORE'S DREAM

UPON the unnumbered sand he lay,
  Where airs of ozone blow ;
His suit was one of Paisley spun,
  His hat was soft and low ;
In the shadow of sleep he traced again
  The Season's torpid flow.

Along the vista of his dreams
  The Lower House appeared ;
Beneath a tile of the beaver's pile
  His comely head he reared ;
The Government was on its feet ;
  The Party faintly cheered.

Again he saw his martial chief
   Address the stolid mace,
Inserting tags of Latin gags
   With elephantine grace ;
The Rads employed their mother tongue,
   And mocked him to his face.

Then in the nick of question time
   Himself adroitly rose ;
Each word that he said came down like lead
   Upon his Leader's toes :
(A tear escaped the sleeper's eye
   And trickled down his nose).

Before him like a hunted thing
   He harried Bryce at bay ;
Then changed the scene to Argentine
   And drew Sir Edward Grey ;

Or sauntered round the crofters' huts,
   And showed Sir George the way.

Now fast and far to Kaffir-land
   His eagle flight he bent ;
Then luffed about and trotted out
   The claims of Welsh dissent ;
While in the nobles' gallery
   The Bishops came and went.

With rare *aplomb* he played the part
   Of truant Labouchere ;
Lashed at the Lords with knotted cords,
   And chaffed the patient Chair ;
From sultry noon to dewy eve
   He never turned a hair.

Though any single innings was
   Comparatively short,

His total *coup* amounted to

    Three columns of report :

(For joy he shifted in his sleep

    And gave a happy snort.)

No fear he felt of wary Whips,

    But made them sick with fright ;

The People's Choice, he raised his voice

    To put the nation right ;

By day he figured in the *Sun*,

    And in the *Star* by night.

Ah ! balmy sleep that thus obscures.

    With kindly irony

The very uncouth and naked truth

    That he was born to be

Plainly a public nuisance or

    A pure nonentity.

            National Observer, September 8, 1894.

.

BEATUS ILLE QUI PROCUL NEGOTIIS

HAPPY the Member that with work in hand

Blithely and buoyantly neglects the same,

Says that the Opposition is to blame,

Discourses of the Upper Chamber, and

Proceeds with airy conscience to vacate.

Remote from toil a peace inviolate

Broods o'er his jocund head with halcyon spell ;

For him no dissonant division bell

Upon an awful sudden sounds the fate

Of his proleptically tepid soup ;

No longer curling round his lissome flanks

The Party Whip adjusts him to the ranks ;

No more he hears the gathering war-whoop—

MacGregor for the Clans ! Redmond for Clare !

Burns for the Masses ! Barclay for the rest !—

Shake the astonied gangway.   Balmy air

Breathes on his brow precisely as supplied

To people in the Islands of the Blest ;

Ripe Autumn courts him on the countryside

Immersed in mildly innocent pursuits ;

There tickles he the ravenous pike, or shoots

A pheasant ere his season ; plucks amain

The pullulating vintage ; lightly sings

Snatches of some sweet topical refrain ;

Smokes freely ; does, in fact, a lot of things

Indicative of pure domestic bliss.

    Nor any evil serpent enters this

Primeval Paradise, save only when

He gathers from the fatuous morning mails

Rumour of one Lloyd-Jonah fearfully,

Down in the deep interior of Wales,

Cursing the bishoprics of Nineveh ;

Or haply hears from wild Hibernian parts

The rattle of shillelaghs on the breeze,

Blent with the throbbing of United Hearts ;

Thanks God devoutly he is not as these,

And prays to be delivered from his friends.

And there are passing moments when he rends

His hair, revolving darkly in his head

What Duties he shall render, being dead.

   Even thus in fitfully heroic rhyme

I meditated, standing at the time

Upon the Bridge of Westminster by night

(A matter of some two and ninety years

Since Wordsworth made remarks upon the site,,

And deemed my thoughts too fine and large for tears :

And so would anyone except his breast

Were hardened to the texture of a brick.

I pictured those who, reckless of arrears,

Being of work deferred now deadly sick,

Reaped, as above, or otherwise, their rest ;

Who drank the waters, took a turn or so

Of easy ambulation on the piers ;

And ceased about the body politic

To care one little solitary blow.

Thames much as usual sauntered to the deep ;

Big Ben observed the quarters ; overhead

The beacon-light was off ; the mace to bed

Had long ago majestically passed ;

Great Scott ! the House of Commons was asleep,

And all its Members wide awake at last !

National Observer, September 22, 1894.

ALLIES IN BLUNDERLAND

(With apologies to Mr. Lewis Carroll)

'You are old, Father William,' the young William said ;
  'We have ceased to accept your advice ;
And yet on our corns you repeatedly tread ;
  Do you think that your conduct is nice ?'

'In my season, Sir William,' the Ancient replied,
  'I was chary of venting my views ;
But now that I'm out of the swim of the tide
  I have done, and shall do, as I choose.'

Said Sir William, ' Of old with the Emerald pack

   You would hunt like a man and a brother :

How is it they've come to a cheque on the track,

   And are having a brush with each other ? '

' In my prime,' said the Ancient, ' I owed 'em a grudge

   And my feelings were deadly to stifle ;

But now that I care not a fig or a fudge,

   Why, I thought I would pay 'em a trifle.'

' On the question of Liquor,' Sir William observed,

   ' Our scheme was erratic, I grant ;

But why from that scheme have you suddenly swerved,

   And protested the thing was a plant ? '

' In the days of my office,' the Ancient explained,

   ' I would wink for the ghost of a vote ;

But now that there's nothing on earth to be gained,

   I have said—well, you saw what I wrote.'

' Just another conundrum, and then I have done—

  Notwithstanding your recent reaction,

I trust you are still to be counted as one

  Of the famous Gladstonian faction ? '

'There is wisdom in years,' was the Ancient's reply ;

  ' And I solemnly hope, if you're spared,

You will cut the connection yourself by-and-by ;

  You would do it at once, if you dared ! '

National Observer, October 6, 1894.

QUIETA NON MOVERE

OF Music Halls let others rant,
  And join the pestilential quarrel,
And glibly answer cant with cant
  As maudlin if not quite so moral ;

Let others, veiled in pseudonyms
  Go pounding on the quest Quixotic
Of novel women's ways and whims,
  Half celibate and half erotic ;

And urge a privilege that is
  Neither original nor recent,
Seeing that most democracies
  Have claimed the right to be indecent ;

Let others swallow day by day
    The last irrefutable story
Of Weh and Yeh, and Japs 'wha hae,'
    And battles singularly gory ;

And lick their lips and magnify
    The growth of European custom,
Judging of Eastern culture by
    Torpedoes and the skill to bust 'em ;—

For me, aweary, I confess,
    Of all the newest things in humour,
Wars, wine and women, art and dress,
    The latest rage, the latest rumour—

How sweet to rest a breathing-while
    Remote from latter-day disputings,
Bradford, beneath thy honoured pile,
    And hear the Premier's dulcet flutings !

And feel that I may rock my brain

  With music of familiar numbers,

That nothing like a novel strain

  Will be allowed to wreck my slumbers.

'Down with the Lords ! Down with the Lords.!'

  I find the harmless iteration

Soothing as some old harpsichord's

  Indifferently dull vibration ;

And while he tunes with easy tact

  His venerable τοῦτ' ἐκεῖνο,

Just how the blessed thing's to act

  I know he knows no more than I know

National Observer, November 3, 1894.

D

PHILADELPHIA; OR, BROTHERLY LOVE

AIR—*Off to Philadelphia*

THE 'Nation' met in Rutland Square,

The rival tickets all were there

To hear the manifesto of McCarthy,

For throughout the recent ructions

He had issued no instructions

For the guidance of the Parliamentary Parthy.

In re the late lamented Whip's

And other Governmental tips,

The Chairman he protested *vi et arte*

    That he never had a notion

    That the same would cause emotion

In the bosom of the Parliamentary Party.

    Though some were spoiling for a fight,

    He hoped sincerely that they might

Appear to be unanimous and hearty,

    Or there wouldn't be a vestige

    Of the old peculiar prestige

Like a halo round the Parliamentary Party.

    No doubt they would be glad to hear

    The Paris funds were floating clear,

And now, with stock in hand on which to start, he

    Would demand a revolution

    In the British Constitution

From the puppets of the Parliamentary Party.

Fair Fortune all across her face.

Was smiling on the Celtic race

From Kerry to the crofters of Cromárty,

And the scene would still be brighter

If the gentle dynamiter

Could be free to join the Parliamentary Party.

.   .   .   .   .

This much they tell, but fail to tell

Just how the swift shillelaghs fell,

What coats were trailed about *civili Marte ;*

For *in camerâ obscurâ*

They had managed to insure a

Privy audit for the Parliamentary Party.

National Observer, November 17, 1894.

THE RECORDING ANGEL, EX-M.P.

[Had the appointment of Mr. Waddy, Q.C., to the Recorder-
ship of Sheffield been postponed a month, the New Register would
then have come into force at the Brigg election, with the result
that the Liberal candidate would have been returned.—*Radical
Press.*]

BRING on the weeping willow,

Wave cypress branches, wave,

And pump a tearful billow

Above the hero's grave ;

Mix, mix the mournful toddy,

And join the wakers' jig,

In memory of Waddy

Q.C. and late of Brigg.

O Waddy ! how we miss you !

   We never knew your worth

Until the fatal issue

   Of your ascent from earth ;

Your passing, as is patent,

   Has brought about a big

Suttee of all the latent

   Electorate of Brigg.

Long years have we been yearning

   To utilise our list

Of occupiers burning

   To have their babies kissed ;

Emancipate and eager,

   The fresh, full-bottomed Whig,

Next month had crushed the leaguer

   And raised the siege of Brigg.

Like Tam o'Shanter's filly,

  We might have fought it out,

And borne our 'chapman billie'

  Beyond the demon rout ;

And forward stoutly straining,

  With never an unpolled twig

Of all our tail remaining,

  Have won the blessed Brig.

Oh, could you but have waited

  One little month at most,

And then been elevated

  To that distinguished post,

Our new Recording Angel,

  Light-hearted as a grig,

Might then have said 'The change'll

  Be barely felt at Brigg.'

Think not we grudge the glory

They deemed your proper due,

We merely grudge the Tory

The place that breathes of you;

And so above your body

A tumulus we dig,

And wail the loss of Waddy

Q.C. and late of Brigg. ·

National Observer, December 15, 1894.

ENTRE NOEL ET LE JOUR DE L'AN

Entre Noël et le Jour de l'An
. The oracles are mostly dumb ;
Still is the hustings' rataplan
    And still the stumper's hideous hum ;
The time invites to eat and drink,
And in the intervals to think.

The statesman's studied repartee
    Is lightly laid upon the shelf ;
Even the Earl of Rosebery
    Refuses to commit himself ;
And having nothing now to say
Has nothing to explain away.

The blessed reign of Santa Claus,

   Symbolic of Domestic Love,

Impels the Radical to pause

   From roaring like a sucking-dove :

A mild and momentary cheer

Resuscitates the panting Peer.

Under the common holly's leaf

   Late foemen fatten cheek by jowl,

The Parish Councils big with beef,

   The Vestries full of Turkey-fowl ;

One equal appetite elates

Progressivists and Moderates.

All party factions pale thier fires,

   Obedient to Christian law ;

Unmitigated calm inspires

The universal British maw ;

And occupies that ample breast

That slumbers in the New Forest.

National Observer, December 29, 1894.

EXUL REDUX

[Sir William Harcourt has returned from the New Forest to his residence in Downing Street.—*Universal Press.*]

WELCOME back from the wilds, O immaculate hermit,
 To regions where sin and society meet ; .
Welcome back from your shady (if so I may term it)
        Retreat.

Far away in the Forest we feel you have rambled
 Through places where natural objects abound ;
With the deer you have coursed, with the rabbits have
  gambolled
        Around.

You have shown an indifference simply sublime to
Affairs that concern the domain of the Guelph,
And have had an improving and nice little time to
Yourself.

You have wandered divinely aloof, independent
Of paltry political ructions and things,
Like an Exile from Erin, a kingly descendant
Of Kings.

Peradventure if faint but intelligent rumours
Have reached you of Rosebery stumping the state,
You have grimly remarked on the fatuous humours
Of fate :

Have observed how his lordship has lately projected
His foot into matters that fitted him·ill,
Not to mention the buskins that *you* were expected
To fill.

Yet the blast of your voice has been hushed to a chirrup,

Your armour reduced to the semblance of silk ;

And the wine of your wrath mitigated with syrup

Or milk.

We have sighed for the shafts of your wit and the cunning

That drew the long bow in the time of your need ;

But your laurels like casual chaff have been running

To seed.

Yes, afar from the fighting, in stately and still ease,

Unmelted of flattery, deaf to dissent,

You have kept in the recognised mode of Achilles

Your tent.

There are murmurs of mutiny openly boasting,

The scent of sedition is borne on the breeze,

Even under our nostrils the Welsher is toasting

His cheese.

O arise from your rest, for our foes are defiant

And half of our comrades are kicking their heels ;

Sally forth like a thundering god or a giant

On wheels.

National Observer, January 12, 1895.

LOWER CHAMBER CONCERT

(BOOK OF WORDS ONLY)

First Voice.

I HAVE thought that the Session should rightly begin
    By a sort of a Radical blast ;
By a Bill that should threaten perdition and shame
To an order of things with a glorious name,
    With a sacred and national past.

And I said, ' I will go for Religion in Wales,
    And in future the title to grace
Shall be kept for Dissenters and Druids and such—
I refer to the people whose tongue is in touch
    With the luminous speech of the race '

Cabinet Chorus.

If *any* scheme deserves to win

Our whole and sole attention,

It is the scheme embodied in

The little Bill you mention.

Second Voice.

I admit that the Welsher is down on the fold

In proportions of fifteen to one,

Having voted for things that he felt were accurst

Till the skin of his conscience is tending to burst,

And his merits are second to none ;

But I plead for the claims of the Land of the League

Where another Commission has sat ;

Though the sides of the question were properly two,

The Commission adopted a different view ;

I've a Bill that is based upon that.

    Chorus : If *any* scheme, &c.

Third Voice.

There is joy in the breach of a personal bond,

But a breach in the State is the best ;

So I stickle for going the integral hog,

And exploding the Union that lies like a log

On the pit of the Liberal chest.

    Chorus : If *any* scheme, &c.

Fourth Voice.

By the way, we have heard that the Party is ripe

(If not rotten) enough for a blow

Of a nature to act as a ram-catapult,

And demolish the Chamber above, and result

    In a Chamber of Horrors below.

    Chorus : If *any* scheme, &c.

        Fifth Voice.

I've a novel design that enables a man

    (And the order is temptingly tall)

To determine, as best he may happen to think,

What and where, and how often, his neighbour may drink,

    Or indeed whether ever at all.

    Chorus : If *any* scheme, &c.

    Sixth to Tenth Voices.

There are matters aloof from ephemeral strife

    That we cannot conceivably chuck,

That affect to its vitals the life of the land,

Such as Toy Locomotives, and Aldermen, and

    Registration and Oysters and Truck !

Chorus.

If *any* schemes deserve to win

Our whole and sole attention,

They are the schemes embodied in

The little Bills you mention.

National Observer, February 9, 1895.

53

SHIFTING SANDS

(THROUGH THE HOUR-GLASS)

AIR—*The sun was shining on the sea*

THE chief was sitting in his place,
  Sitting with all his might ;
He did his very best to keep
  His banner out of sight ;
And this was odd when he was in
  The middle of the fight.

J. R. was fuming sulkily ;
  He thought the bloody fray

Had got no business to proceed
    Another blessed day,
Unless the army chose to own
    That Erin blocked the way.

The House was full as full could be,
    The leaders sick as sick ;
They threw a little dirt about,
    In hope that some would stick ;
They also backed a heap of bills ;
    They often go on tick.

The Asquith and the Labouchere
    Were looking round the land,
The former laughed aloud to see
    Such quantities of sand ;
' If we could plough it up a bit,'
    He said, ' it *would* be grand !

'If all the Party in a row
　　Ploughed it for half a year,
I 'wonder if it would affect
　　A solitary Peer.'
'I doubt it,' said the Radical,
　　And smiled from ear to ear.

'Still, *if* you think the ploughing might
　　Annoy the Landed Class,
My little lot will lend itself
　　To bring the scheme to pass ;
I call it fairly asinine,
　　But—"write me down an ass !" '

'The time has come,' the Asquith said,
　　'To talk of bogus bills ;
Of Welsh dissent and questions like
　　The cure of Tenants' ills ;

And whether Mr. Morley knows

  Of any patent pills.

' We thank you therefore very much

  For being really nice,

And kindly promising to play

  The ass at any price.'

' I don't see where the oyster beds

  Come in,' said Mr. Bryce.

National Observer, February 23, 1895.

THE BATTLE OF LONDON

Air—*Hohenlinden*

On London, where the gas was low,
And still as winter was the flow
Of water-companies that go
    On piling money rapidly,

The counters counting up the votes—
This side the sheep, and that the goats—
Were making speculative notes
    On what the net result would be.

But London saw another scene

When those that hate the happy mean

Were gathered round the fatal screen

To welcome their majority ;

That sight was better than a play—

The Radical *Hetæria*

All in their caravanserai,

And ripe for any revelry !

But when the tape began to click,

The sanguine body politic

Became incontinently sick,

And cursed aloud Progressively ;

And watching half the weary night

The swift recording demon write

The list of fallen in the fight,

A sorry tale of twenty-three,

They said it was a marvel that
A pampered Proletariat
Should treat the labelled Democrat
    As if he were the enemy.

But in the subsequent debate
They made as if to mock at fate ;
The language was Immoderate,
    It also was extempore.

But fuller yet the bitter bowl,
When Monday gave the perfect poll,
And Wandsworth bells began to toll
    O'er Dickinson his sepulchree.

Save, Hutton, half thy banners, save
For winding-sheets to wrap the brave !
And let Sir George above their grave
    Lift up his wail Tit-Bitterly.

But as for Johnny, by-and-by,

He'll talk to those that wiped his eye,

And then, my word, there'll be a high

Auld ' nicht wi' Burns ' in Battersea !

National Observer, March 9, 1895.

DISCRETA SEDES

By what is technically called ' to-day'

 They will perhaps have settled on a Speaker ;

If so, the thing or two I had to say

 Is bound to be proportionately weaker ;

It is a little galling to the mind

 To cut a thoughtful and prophetic caper,

And get the wrong result a day behind ;

 But that's the beauty of a weekly paper.

Under the circumstances I prefer

 To make reflections rather than to prophesy ;

And let me say that it would not occur

 To *me* to seek the post ; it is an office I

Consider full of dignity and grace,

    But then there's precious little else to show for it ;

And when you come to think about the case

    It's odd that such a lot of people go for it.

To sleep ! perchance to eat !   You must allow

    These blessings are a natural tradition ;

A really healthy creature like a cow

    Will often do the two in one position ;

But though his need be exquisitely sore,

    A Speaker cannot properly do either,

At any rate from three to twelve (or more)

    He barely gets the semblance of a breather.

Through all the drowsy boredom of debates

    He still must keep a counterfeit composure,

Look callous when a person perorates,

    And know precisely when to put the closure :

For each enigma have its fit reply,

    Weigh well his judgment lest it prove erroneous,

Give every man his ear and some his eye,

    And do his duty by the late Polonius.

Through oratory seldom quite sublime

    He shows, as I observed, a mild urbanity,

Says 'Order ! order !' at the proper time,

    And checks the Government from mere profanity ;

He has to know his precedent by rote,

    Distinguish when the Serjeant should be sent for,

Do anything except record his vote—

    The only thing a Member's rightly meant for.

All which considered, were the choice my own,

    I'd have my dearest enemy appointed ;

There was indeed a rumour faintly blown

    Suggesting that Sir William be anointed :

By blood a Prince, he knows the regal art ;

    'That chair would be his throne, and he the soul of it ;

And while another man might fill the part,

    I'm fairly certain *he* would fill the whole of it !

There are that look, but luckily in vain,

    For him, the Unforgotten-of-the-million,

The Grander, Older, Man to come again

    Like Arthur from the shadows of Avilion ;

While others ask, by Justice with the scales,

    Why Englishmen should be the only starters ;

Is this a further slight to gallant Wales,

    And yet another knock for Erin's martyrs ?

I rather fancy some heroic shape,

    All swollen with a patriot's emotion,

Our own Alpheus or the cultured Snape

    To represent the Mistress of the Ocean ;

And if he were a Member, I surmise

The Ministry would have another-rank lark,

And enter Mr. Redford for the prize

In view of his experience as a bank clerk.

National Observer, March 23, 1895.

A COCK AND BULL STORY

AIR—*Casabianca*

['European navies were like fighting cocks, armed to the teeth ;
a single spark might cause an explosion.'—*Dr. MacGregor on the
Navy Estimates.*]

THE fighting cock stood on the deck,
His eye was rolling red,
His feathers whiffled round his neck,
His crest was on his head.

He wore his spur above his heel,
His claws were underneath,
He also had a mass of steel
Plate armour on his teeth.

Meanwhile the House was haggling on
  In one of those debates
When Little England jumps upon
  The Navy Estimates.

There Cleophas, of many wiles,
  Brought up his little lot,
And Mr. Byles, with wreathéd smiles,
  Was deadly on the spot.

And Labby said the bootless pay
  Of navies should be stamped on ;
' There is no boot ! ' as strikers say
  In Labby's own Northampton.

' Then came a burst of thunder-sound '
  That shook the very street,
And lo ! MacGregor's form was found
  To be upon its feet.

He called the rates a great expense,

    He was a peaceful Scot,

And said the talk about ' defense '

    Was simply Tommy-rot.

Far better for his country's good,

    So long allowed to bleed,

If only half the money could

    Be spend across the Tweed.

Then with a petrifying shout,

    Like some *clamantis vox*;

He fetched a trumpet note about

    The teeth of fighting cocks ;

A simile of crew and crew

    All ripe for any ruction

(Refer to verses one and two,

    Or else the introduction) ;

A spark might fall from out the sea,

  Completely unforeboded,

And then the birds—where would they be ?

  Why, they would be exploded.

He looked around for some applause

  From front or side or rear ;

They never said a word, because

  They hadn't strength to cheer.

With many an accidental jest

  The hearts of men were full,

But O ! the thing they liked the best

  Was bold MacGregor's bull !

Punch, April 6, 1895.

HOW LONG, O LORD? HOW LONG?

In Calverley's delightful pages
   I often chortle at the view
Expressed by that supreme of sages
   About a certain cockatoo
Embellished with a regal tuft,
And suitable for being stuffed.

I like the creature's insolent
   Ability to recognise
How much his owner's heart was bent
   On his immediate demise ;
And yet he winked the other eye,
And stolidly refused to die.

There is a strong and quite absurd

    Resemblance, as it seems to me,

Between the tricks of Blades's bird

    And those of Harcourt's Ministry ;

In each we trace a constitution

Inimical to dissolution.

But *à propos* of winged things,

    And passing from the cockatoo,

The fancy naturally springs

    To what a swan is said to do ;

They say, when dying in a ditch,

He sings a hymn at concert pitch.

To grapple with the parallel—

    The humour of the passing fowl

Suggests that we may very well

    Remark in this stupendous howl

Emitted by the Anti-Clerics

A sort of moribund hysterics.

I know a book by Mr. Barrie,

    An early. work that should be read

By people who incline to tarry,   ·

    Well knowing they are *Better Dead ;*

I wish to. have a copy sent

To all the present Government.

For as the work that they have done

    Was long ago precisely nil,

And since the Session has begun

    Is something rather smaller still,

It seems the best they can achieve

Is just to give it up and leave. .

What frequently will happen in

The history of any man

Addicted to a course of sin

Applies to them ; for nothing can

In all their life—as I'm a prophet—

Become them like the leaving of it.

National Observer, April 6, 1895.

THE UNION OF HEARTS

[' To-day we feel, without scarce (*sic*) knowing why, a desire to
cheer for Umra Khan ; who, amid the rocks and cliffs of Chitral, is
giving battle to English regiments.'—*United Ireland.*]

WHEN the legions of Umra are dancing

Well out of the way of the ' Guides,'

And the pick of the Lancers are lancing

Whatever is left of their hides ;

When from every available station

The bullets are beating like rain—

He has this consolation

That some of our nation

Are backing his Plan of Campaign,

Umra Khan and his Plan of Campaign.

Though the seas roll gurly between,

There's a party that wears the green,

A brotherly band

That stretches a hand

To the foes of the State and the Queen.

When the Speaker affair was decided,

And Radicals cared not a fig

For the matter of merit, provided

That one of them went for the wig ;

When their candidate noticed the grim

Iteration of Healy's refrain,

How delightful for him

To remember that Tim

Was supporting his Plan of Campaign,

The Speakership Plan of Campaign !

When the Leader is sworn to agree to

   The sack of the labourer's club,

While neglecting the option to veto

   The National Liberal Pub ;

Then O'Brien suggests with a smile

   That, so long as they needn't abstain

      In a similar style

      On the Emerald Isle,

   They will vote for his Plan of Campaign,.

   For Sir William, his Plan of Campaign.

When the chief of the firm of freebooters

   Is stalking the Anglican fold,

And conducting his secular looters

   In quest of a quarry of gold ;

When he sees that the Church's subjection

   Is chiefly Papistical gain—

And the ' National' section

From Roman affection

Are pushing his Plan of Campaign,

The Dissenter, his Plan of Campaign ;—

Then it makes an harmonious scene,

For there is really nothing between

His hand and the hands

Of the party that stands

By the foes of the State and the Queen.

National Observer, April 20, 1895.

A TIED HOUSE

WE are sons of the soil where the usquebaugh blooms

      And the scent of its fumes

      Is as healthy as tar ;

      And we miss our poteen

      In the Saxon shebeen

Where they serve us across the Imperial Bar.

Chorus : For the potion to which we aspire

      Is a blending of whisky and fire,

      But they've cheapened our cheer

      To the smallest of beer,

    And we're tied to Sir William's Entire.

We emerged from the sylvan recesses of Blarney,

> From Cork and Killarney,
>
> From Louth and Tyrone,
>
> With the ultimate notion
>
> Of passing a motion

For having a House and a Bar of our own.

When they brewed the Dissenters an unction to ease 'em,

> We bargained to please 'em
>
> By taking it hot ;
>
> Though the mark of the robber
>
> And brand of the jobber

Were burnt on the barrel and punched on the pot.

When they served a Lawsonian syrup to follow,

> We managed to swallow
>
> The nauseous treat ;

Though our veteran gorges

Rebelled at these orgies

And sighed for a sip of the usual, neat.

But the latest of all is a singular brand

For reviving the land

When it comes to the vote ;

It's a popular bribe

That we've got to imbibe

On the principle known as One Party One Throat.

There's a cup that is filling (and still in arrears)

For the Chamber of Peers,

As the wages of sin ;

Which is fruity, no doubt,

But we fail to make out

Where The Nation (that's Us) is supposed to come in.

We have lain pretty low, but the lowliest worm

      Is permitted to squirm

      On a question of thirst ;

      If he can't be supplied

      In a House that is tied,

Why, the knot must be severed or something will burst.

Chorus : For the potion to which we aspire

      Is a blending of whisky and fire,

      But they've cheapened our cheer

      To the smallest of beer,

      And we're tied to Sir William's Entire.

National Observer, May 4, 1895.

G

'*THEY BORE HIM BAREFACED ON THE BIER*'

OPHELIA

['Much excitement was produced in the Lobby by Sir William
Harcourt's intimation that the present Budget would, in all pro-
bability, be his last.'—*Daily Press.*]

O LOYAL friends ! O gallant foes !

O quite a lot of other factions !

This is, as not a creature knows,

The last of all my Budget actions ;

For though I don't propose to run away,

I still refuse to fight another day.

Long since, I had it in my heart

To break this parlous piece of news,

And cause a momentary start

    Among the sleepers in their pews ;

For I have felt—of course I may be wrong—

That lately I have not been going strong.

All flesh is grass—or so they say—

    And certainly the time must come

When heroes undergo decay,

    And even princely lips are dumb ;

We all must ultimately yield our place,

Sooner or later—later in my case.

Nor could I find a fitter hour

    In which to shadow forth my fall,

That none may weep my waning power,

    Or turn his face toward the wall

(If anybody really wants to sob, he

Will please to go and do it in the Lobby) ;

For while I grasp the Budget Bill,
  With swelling chest and chin sublime,
To many friends my posture will
  Recall the splendour of my prime ;
And even Envy owns, at such a minute,
That nobody beside myself is in it.

What fitter hour, again, than this
  For Erin's sons to learn the cost
Of all that they are like to miss
  With yet another Leader lost,
Whose latest joy it is to do a bit
Of Budget-cooking for their benefit ?

For when my ashes shall be cool
  They'll think : ' He laughed a little at
Our homely taste for local rule,
  But in the end he noticed that

The extra whisky duty gave us pain,

And so he kindly took it off again.'

'Then toll for me the passing gong,

   And lightly heave my body hence,

And sing me fair Ophelia's song,

   And say : ' It truly was immense

To see him settle down, without a tear,

Barefaced, as ever, on the British Beer ! '

World, May 8, 1895.

A NATIONAL LIBERAL 'BEANO'

THERE was a noise of revelry by night,
  And England's Radicals had gathered there
In all their practically Peerless might ;
  The Independent Labour Party's hair
Was curled ; and Beauty, with her best attire on,
Recalled the *Eve of Waterloo* (by Byron).

Soft eyes were seen to droop, high hearts to bound,
  And all went merry as a grig—when hush !
When hark ! a deep and soul-seducing sound
  Came pealing through the careless, giddy crush ;
Was it the trombone, or the supper bell,
Or else the voice of some 'voluptuous swell' ?

O mellow organ ! skilled alike to make

    The Proletariat glow with speechless glee ;

To keep sublimely and sublimely break

    The torpid spell of taciturnity ;

Or haply in the humour of romance

To sound the invitation to the dance !

Is this the voice that lately, sweet and low,

    Checked off the profits of the passing year,

And sought with fair persuasiveness to show

    The National advantages of Beer,

Implying that it were a cruel shame

To put a Local stopper on the same ?

Is this the voice whose sad appealing note

    Prognosticated imminent demise,

Much like the swan that tunes his parched throat

    Almost immediately before he dies ?

That now with high elation drowns the dirge
In pæans on the sheer volcano's verge?

The same, but not the same ; the scene is changed ;
   The hour invites to badinage and bluster,
When round him all his own elect are ranged,
   Save those, a negligeable few, that muster
Where rival lips—in quite another room—
Defiantly postpone the day of doom.

I would I had been there ; by all report
   It was a little heaven below to see ,
The Nonconformist Welsher take his sport
   Unfettered, reckless, dissolutely free ;
Indeed, I always understood his tone is
A little loose at conversaziones.

But when the leading wags had plied their wit,

  The lucubrated jest, the jaunty trope,

And proved the Ministry were nice and fit,

  And he, the Leader, full of spring and hope,

O then to see him join the dance, and go

Revolving on the trim elastic toe !

Such are the scenes of bliss without alloy

  That captivate the People's throbbing breast,

The episodes of pure domestic joy

  That fairly thrill the chaste suburban chest ;

The distant province hears the happy hum,

And murmurs—Lo ! Millennium is come !

World, May 15, 1895.

'BIRTH'S INVIDIOUS BAR'

AIR—*Lady Clare*

IT was the time when Budgets blow,
  And talk of Beer was in the air ;
Lord Wolmer sat him in a row
  Behind the back of Labouchere.

I trow the latter saw his chance,
  Your Radical, you may be sure,
Is ever eager to advance
  The claims of Primogeniture.

He noticed—if report was true—
  A noble Earl of high degree
Established in a common pew
  In ordinary company,

The Earl in question, closely pressed
  About his name and natal star,
Somewhat denied, somewhat confessed,
  And gently bowing crossed the Bar.

Up came the Leader on the spot,
  He wished to make the matter clear,
Either his honoured friend was not,
  Or else he was, a Belted Peer.

The thing could soon be worried out,
  Meanwhile the claimant might receive
The benefit of any doubt,
  And, so to put it, take his leave.

It never was permitted by
   The rules of reason or of rhyme
For any man to occupy
   Two several places at a time.

No one could simply say, 'I please
   To sit in both ;' it wouldn't do ;
Although a Member, if obese,
   Might cover ground enough for two.

And similarly, though a man
   At times might run to double chins,
No decent Æthiopian
   Had ever worn a brace of skins.

' Nay now,' said Mr. Chamberlain,
   ' To sit or not to sit : this is
The weary question once again
   Of Peerage disabilities.'

'Nay now, what question?' said the Chair,
  'What motion? nay, I know of none.'
The Chief assumed his martial air ;
  'You want a motion? here is one :—

'The noble lord is bound to sit
  Elsewhere by virtue of his status ;
I move the making of a writ
  To rectify the rude hiatus.

'Who dares oppose himself to me
  Is ill-advised ; his words are light.'
'Nay now,' that other said, 'but see,
  You show a naughty, naughty spite.

'Until he prove his right of race,
  According to your own admission
The Earl is beltless, and his case
  Is merely one of grave suspicion.'

The Leader's logic grew severe
    And exquisitely pertinent—
' If he aspires to be a Peer,
    But not a Lord of Parliament—

' If he aspires to be a Peer
    But claims to sit within the Bar,
Where are we ?   Neither there nor here,
    In fact, we dunno where we are !'

National Observer, May 18, 1895.

A LAMENT FOR THE MACGREGOR

HE's gane ! he's gane ! he's frae us torn,

The brawest billie e'er was born ;

Mourn, feckless Caledonia ! mourn,

   Ye Whigs an' a' !

Macgregor's left the Hous' forlorn,

   Rob Roy's ava' !

Ye buckies by the braes o' Ness,

When ye obsairve the Tory press

Sae fu' o' glee, wi' dour distress

   Your wames mun ache ;

We're in an awfu' sickly mess,

   An' nae mistake !

Our chiel was aye a shinin' licht,
An' when he spak wi' a' his micht
The Hous' wad keckle at the sicht,
        An' brust wi' laughter ;
The timmers shuk ae blessed nicht
        Frae floor to rafter !

That nicht he rose in fechtin' mood
Ahint the Chieftain's fearfu' brood,
An' hitcht his sporan up an' stood
        An' straikt his kilt,
An' ilka body thocht that bluid
        Wad soon be spilt.

' Is there,' said he, 'ae canny Scot
But feels his marrow meltin' hot

To see the Crofters gae to pot

An' pure perdeetion

A' thro' the blazin' Tammy-rot

O' yon Commeesion ?

' I'd hae ye ken I stand at bay !

Noo will ye gie the clans a day?'

Auld Willie winked—' I canna say ;

I sairly doot it ;

Gin I were you I wadna lay

Lang odds aboot it.'

Macgregor snuffed the air a wee,

An' tuk an aith to do or dee,

Then oot he spak wi' gleamin' e'e

An' gloomin' braw—

' It isna gude enough for me ! '

An' walked awa'.

H

He's gane ! the cantiest o' leeches,

An' eke as gleg at makin' speeches

As ony meenister wha preaches

        The proven word,

An' we abode amang our breaches,

        An' never stirred !

For verra shame our beardies brissle,

An' Scotland's greetin' ower her thrissle

To think we daurtna lift a miss'le

        Against her faes ;

Ae thing remains—to wet our whissle.

        An' droon our waes.

Then gar the whisky glasses clink,

An' tak a tearfu' stoup o' drink,

An' mourn wi' us the missin' link

   O' Scotland's weal ;

Our billie's gi'en us a' a jink,

   An' that's the de'il !

National Observer, June 1, 1895.

INTERMEZZO

(WHITSUNTIDE)

Now doff we winter's weeds, for May is out,.
   And June is in with eager, freckled face ;
And here are trippers tripping all about
      The place.

They take a short recess, as I suppose,
   From choice, or fashion, or the force of wont ;
And those that work recede as well as those
      That don't.

Even the faithful Commons turn aside

From legislating for a little bit,

. And freely wanton in the flowing tide

Of Whit.

The very Speaker ceases now to speak,

And hushed is each intolerable Bore ;

The mace is put in wadding for a week

Or more.

A solemn stillness, as the poet says,

Holds all the atmosphere ; the cheery char

Hums reverently as she polishes

. The Bar.

The Mice of Parliament in measured tone

Discuss a little subterranean Bill ;

The fearless beetle wanders at his own

Sweet will

Emancipated from the heavy task
Of really doing nothing all the while,
The House with one consent proceeds to bask
And smile.

One common jubilee corrects their spleen,
One touch of Nature unifies the lot,
And any trifling difference is clean
Forgot.

Together as they plough the driven sand,
Securely bunkered on the breezy links,
An augur sees a rival augur, and
He winks.

The weanéd infant and the cocatrice
Fracture their bulgers on the self-same tee;
Such harmony is very, very nice
To see.

Homesick and heartsick, to its proper lair

The slighted, blighted band of Erin sails ;

The Welshers, on the other hand, repair

To Wales.

And Weir's awa' with all his kilted crew

To greet MacGregor on his native heath,

And rouse the rebel clans, and arm 'em to

The teeth.

The Chief, in some New Forest glade reclined,

Extemporises immemorial jokes,

Or quaintly carves them on the listening rind

·Of oaks.

And courtly Cleophas takes heart of grace

To think the People own at least a Peer

Who anyhow can win one Derby race

A year.

God bless the happy creatures !   As for me,

Why dwell, I say, upon the paltry past ?

This little holiday is like to be

Their last.

World, June 5, 1895.

FAREWELL TO CORK

Now toll the temporary bell
For W. O'Brien's knell ;
I come, in fact, to say farewell,
    O Cork !

Politically, as you know,
I've grappled with our common foe ;
Now Chance has been and laid me low,
    O Cork !

I've sat, a hunted thing, in ditches ;

I've served a spell in prison, which is

A place where people steal your breeches,

O Cork !

I said, ' No matter ! let 'em take

My trousers for my country's sake,

Bare legs do not a prison make,'

O Cork !

Then, ere I won the light of day,

An enemy had smirched with clay

•Another part of my array,

O Cork !

That garment which I never fail

On any lightest hint to trail—

A Peer had trodden on its tail,

O Cork !

I flung my gage ; without a fear

For any costs, however dear,

I battled with the bloated Peer,

O Cork !

But ah ! it was a brother Celt

That planted bruisers on my pelt,

And hit me underneath the belt,

O Cork !

My own familiar friend who laid

His hand in mine and offered aid,

And wanted, later, to be paid,

O Cork !

A son of Erin ! shame, I say ;

He might have known before to-day

That Erin's patriots *never pay*,

O Cork !

I wonder how he had the face
To thus defy, to thus disgrace
The high traditions of his race,
    O Cork !

He'll question next the League's intent,
And hint that money might be spent
From time to time in paying rent !
    O Cork !

How could he let his fellow-man,
Who preached with him the pious Plan,
Lie stricken like a pelican,
    (O Cork !)

That welters in the waste alone,
A shaft embedded in his bone,
Whose feathers were his very own ?
    O Cork !

Enough ! it makes me deadly sick ;
And there's the *Irish. Catholic*
Engaged in heaving half a brick,
    O Cork !

I'll tell Timotheus what I mean
When once we meet on College Green
With new shillelaghs, nice and clean,
    O Cork !

Meanwhile it might be just as well
To toll the temporary bell
For W. O'Brien's knell,
    O Cork !

                National Observer, June 15, 1895.

WE ARE MINUS SEVEN

A GOVERNMENT, dear Editor,
　That drew so scant a breath
Would seem to be intended for
　A rather early death.

I met a stickit Ministry,
　It was but three years old,
Already on its brow were sprent
　Grey hairs among the gold.

Its health, I thought, was far from good,

    Its weight exceeding light ;

I greatly wondered how it could

    Have sat so very tight.

' Your surplus voters, free or paid—

    How many may you be ? '

' We reckon seven in all,' it said,

    And slowly winked at me.

' A sorry margin,' I replied,

    ' It surely has decreased ;

I quite supposed that you relied

    On forty odd, at least.'

' O ! half a pair has gone away

    To Kiel, across the sea ;

And some have joined, we grieve to say,

    The great minority.

'The Parnellites have snapped the link,

    Macgregor's o'er the Border,

And one is shaky on the drink,

    And Gully's keeping order.

'And round the churchyards one in ten:

    Tunes up his private organ,

And Osborne Morgan now and then

    Dissents from Osborne Morgan.

'For one the widowed Cork's lament

    Is daily growing louder,

And one has lately had his tent

    Blown up with smokeless powder.

'And one, among the first to go,

    A Whip of gentle cords—

He left us sorrowing below,

    And mounted to the Lords.

' And often, Sir, when all was blue,
　　And work was in arrears,
For want of better things to do,
　　We sat and cursed the Peers.

'We sat and planted Bill on Bill,
　　We stuck, and wouldn't stir,
And every evening things were still
　　Precisely what they were.

'We ploughed the ocean's sandy bed,
　　We filled the foaming cup,
Or knocked a statue on the head
　　Before we put it up.

'At last there came a deadly rot ;
　　Beneath a blazing heaven
We lost our little racing lot,
　　And trickled down to seven !

'Who would have thought that Ascot week

   Should prove our dissolution—

The straw that shattered, so to speak,

   The camel's constitution ? '

'But still, with seven braves,' I said,

   'A deal may yet be done ;

Your Derby chief, as I have read,

   Would be content with *one* !'

'O ! we could do a deal or two

   With seven,' it replied ;

'The only thing that troubles us

Is this—it isn't on the plus,

   But on the minus side.'

World, June 26, 1895.

·

IN ROSEBERII MEMORIAM

(The Old Man epilogises in the Miltonic manner)

YET once more, O my Party, yea, once more

(This time with health as hardy as a rock

Through my excursus to a foreign shore),

I seek you as a mother seeks her flock

And finds the pretty creatures plucked and bare.

Bitter occasion and a shattered pair

Compel me thus above an honoured bier

To perpetrate the unaccustomed rhyme ;

For Rosebery is gone, gone ere his prime,

Poor Rosebery, and never hurt a Peer !

We two were nursed upon the selfsame bills,

And fed the selfsame foolish bounding sheep,

Though he has never known the care that kills

The lowly commoner ; nor sighed for sleep

What time Sir William wound his sultry horn,

Or rash Alpheus rolled his turgid stream

Battening upon the dews of early morn ;

Or pompous Ughtred argued his supreme

Enlightenment on matters of the main ;

Nor would the Irish pipes omit to moan,

Tempered to the Scottish screel,

Nor braw MacGregor leave his local reel,

Nor 'Tanner cease from motions all his own ;

Nor from the wake would Tim be absent long,

He often would oblige us with a song.

But O the heavy change now thou art gone !

Now thou art gone and fairly in thy urn

And not at present likely to return !

As killing as the pace of Isinglass

(*Emeritus* and gathered to his stud),

So shows the canker-worm that nipped, alas !

Our Primrose in the bud.

What fittest bard shall frame thy benison ?

Shall doubting Thomas at a venture tune

The Cambrian harp, or Allen loose his lays,

Or flippant Labouchere

With that divinely supercilious air

Assuage the pestilential heat of June

By damning thee with faint and frigid praise ?

Where were ye, traitors, when the Tory's teeth

Closed o'er the open throat of Rosebery ?

For either ye were plunging on the Heath,

Where he hath often sported, free from care,

Or munching unaware

The toothsome shrimp with your domestic tea.

Ah me ! what boots it with incessant zeal

To ply the paltry politician's trade,

And strictly educate a thankless land?

Were it not better far, as I have done,

To chuck the thing betimes and leave the sun,

And toy with high old Homer in the shade,

Or trip with Currie's little lot to Kiel,

Or do, like thee, the double Derby trick?

Far better this than thus to simply stick

And plough the unremunerative sand.

O fount of Local Veto's stream !   O pump

Of Lawson's limpid-lapsing eloquence !

Not thine it was to sink that sacred Rump,

Although I freely ween

That with a little luck it might have been.

Nay, nay, it was the Opposition's low

And fatal lust for national defence

That dealt the irremediable blow,

I know.

But see the mourners at the coffin's edge,

Each shepherd with his own peculiar bill,

Good honest John with literary quill,

And shamrock, out of season, at his breast,

Weeping—'Ah, who hath reft my dearest pledge?'

And there with duplicated grief oppressed

The rudely disestablished Asquith mopes,

A steeple-hat upon his drooping crest,

And wails with double pipe because of twins.

A little for his registration hopes,

But most he sorrows for his country's sins,

That they, the pastors that defend the fold,

Should leave the single-hearted wolf without

To famish in the cold.

But check, my shepherds, check the mournful rout ;

For Rosebery is not precisely gone :

He still remains the Genius of the Turf ;

And this is but a temporary change.

In my comparatively varied range

I too have tossed on Fortune's fickle surf ;

And I have also known

Opinions rudely veer in many a man ;

For instance, I was once Gladstonian.

So sang the hoary swain and bade adieu ;

To-morrow to fresh themes and pamphlets new.

National Observer, June 29, 1895.

PRINTED BY

SPOTTISWOODE AND CO., NEW-STREET SQUARE

LONDON

HORACE AT CAMBRIDGE.

3s. 6d. net.

. 'A delightful little book of light verse. . . . To every university man, and particularly of course to Cambridge men, this book will be a rare treat. But in virtue of its humour, its extreme and felicitous dexterity of workmanship both in rhyme and metre, and the aptness of its allusions, it will appeal to a far wider public. I pledge Mr. Seaman in a bumper of College Audit ! and beg him to give us more of his work.'   PUNCH.

'" Horace at Cambridge " is a volume of sprightly verses . . . . The adaptation is often felicitous, the humour is bright and spontaneous, and the several metres are skilfully handled.'   TIMES.

'In the pages of the "Granta" . . . his clever and diverting Horatian verses began to delight us. . . . The novelty of Mr. Seaman's odes and songs lies chiefly in the skilful adaptation of the Horatian point of view to Cambridge life and current topics of the day.'
                                                        SATURDAY REVIEW.

' By his book "Horace at Cambridge," Mr. Owen Seaman has conclusively established his right to be rated as A. B. among university poets. . . . He treats Cambridge and its pursuits with a humour which is always sprightly and refreshing. . . . His odes possess a very high literary quality, and his adaptations are as felicitous as his metres and rhymes are apt and clever. . . . We very cordially recommend Mr. Seaman's book not only to all university men, but to all who are likely to care for verse which is not unworthy to be ranked with the efforts of Calverley the immortal.'   WORLD.

'" Horace at Cambridge " . . . should have attractions for all who can appreciate genuine humour as expressed in neat and sprightly measures. . . . Throughout his slender work Mr. Seaman is a diverting companion. His style has much variety and considerable finish.'
                                                        GLOBE.

' In the pretty volume entitled " Horace at Cambridge," Mr. Seaman may be congratulated upon having followed with considerable success in the footsteps of the late C. S. C. . . . The majority of these amusing pieces are directly " drawn from Cambridge scenes or associa-

tions " . . . There is a distinctly Horatian flavour about them. . . .
As a rhymester Mr. Seaman is usually extremely felicitous, and he
manages his ingenious metres with unfailing skill.'   ATHENÆUM.

'Mr. Seaman's " Horace at Cambridge " has wit and gaiety. . . .
It is never slipshod ; it has the neatness, the precision, the sparkle of
its Latin namesake.'   .   SPEAKER.

'Mr. Seaman . . . is the Juvenal of every seedy decadent, and the
author of " A Ballad of a Bun." He has also, *inter alia*, made the
most ingenious " Plea for Trigamy " on record, and he is the Horace
of the "Granta" . . . Each poem is based upon some well-known
ode of Horace, brought up to date, transferred into the latest of rhythms,
decked with the gayest of rhymes. . . .'   PALL MALL GAZETTE.

'A volume of bright, clever verses. . . .'   DAILY CHRONICLE.

'The fun is distinctly good and laughter-moving.'
            .   WESTMINSTER GAZETTE.

'Mr. Seaman has a light hand and a pretty wit.'
                       SKETCH.

' " O. S." are initials well known in more than one contemporary.
. . . There is a good deal of clever verbal jugglery in " Horace at
Cambridge," and Mr. Seaman's rhymes are always neat.'
                       VANITY FAIR.

'Here is a genuine treat for all lovers of *jeux d'esprit*. The book
is exceedingly clever. . . . Mr. Seaman's muse is first cousin to those
of Calverley, Canning, and Praed.'   .   THE LIBERAL.

'After Mr. Anstey, perhaps there is no one writing at present who
combines so successfully the frequently incongruous elements of wit and
literature. . . . Mr. Seaman is a genuine humorist, and among those
who have borne the " sacred flame of persiflage from Cambridge
portals" he must always hold a popular position, taking rank as no
unworthy follower of Praed and of Calverley.'   SUN.

'Mr. Seaman's wonderful dexterity and ease of rhyme and manner
can perhaps be fully appreciated only by those who have themselves
attempted to write light verse ; for his is pre-eminently the art which
conceals artifice, and things of this kind seem so desperately easy to pen
until you make the attempt for yourself.'   GRANTA.

A. D. INNES & CO., Bedford Street, London.

www.ingramcontent.com/pod-product-compliance
Lightning Source LLC
Chambersburg PA
CBHW030614270326
41927CB00007B/1172